I Meant to Tell You

# I Meant to Tell You

*poems*

Noona O'Riley

WESTERN EYE PRESS

2017

I MEANT TO TELL YOU
*is published by*
*Western Eye Press,*
*a small independent publisher*
*(very small, and very independent)*
*with a home base in the Colorado Rockies*
*and an office in Sedona Arizona.*
I Meant to Tell You *is also*
*available as an eBook*
*in various formats.*

*© 2017 Noona O'Riley*
*Western Eye Press*
*P O Box 1008*
*Sedona, Arizona 86339*
*1 800 333 5178*
*www.WesternEyePress.com*

*First edition, 2017*
*ISBN 13   978-0-941283-45-8*

*cover photo by the author*
*photo of the poet by John Reeves*

DEAR READER

These poems were created in the bardic tradition of speaking them into being, often in the dark hours of the night. Most of them were never written down prior to the making of this book, but lived in my memory.

They are always best spoken.


ABOUT THE AUTHOR

Noona O'Riley is a poet, visual artist, and fabric artist, living in the Sangre de Cristo mountains of southern Colorado. She inherited her love of poetry from her mother, Jean Young Brunk, an enthusiastic teacher of writing and literature. Her poems are shaped by listening to the sounds and cadence of the words; by the inner prompting to get it just right, to be as true as possible to the inspiration; and always to leave room for a happy accident.


THANKS

to Lito Tejada-Flores for designing this book; to Joann Reeves and Linde Waidhofer for careful reading and editing; to Martin Macaulay for taming the computer files; to Sheila Ramsey, Linda Craig, and Esther Jantzen for their great encouragement; to the town of Crestone, and the landscape of mountains and valley; and especially to my dear family and friends for inspiring every word.

*for*
*Gwen, Jono, and Max*

# CONTENTS

## NIGHT WALKER

tonight I am night walker
cousin to the stars
my body neither full nor empty
moves like vapor in the air
the night is filled with evening prayers

without even knowing why
you may fall into a longing
you had no idea was there
tiny crystal spiders
will come move you down a path
the end, a vast horizon,
is merely a beginning

you'll be like me
night walker
vapor in the air
your hair is full of prayers.

for some of us it take the longest time
to even want
to know ourselves
the idea comes quietly
an afterthought, an aside
amidst the more important activities of our lives
it's almost sweet
the face of a flower, of a weed
that grows beside the outside faucet
where we go to water
the more important flowers of our garden
the ones who scandalize us with color
pinks and gold
the ones to whom we go for
baptism
in their blue perfume
and then the weed
we notice it much as we might notice
a scrap of paper that has fallen from our pocket
and bending down to pick it up
curious
although expecting nothing much

for some of us it takes the longest time
to harvest the magnitude
of noticing the weed.

Canadian geese are migrating
all over the valley sky this morning
as I drive into town
streams of them everywhere
like nets cast up to catch the sky
cranes too
cranes are flying in
their long Egyptian necks
great lapping wings
that plow and fold and plow
the heavy air
I must be part crane part sky
this migration is as familiar to my body
as waking each morning
alone in bed
to the rise and falling of my breath

last night on TV I watched Denzel Washington
move like a panther, pantherman,
down the streets at night
seizing from the darkness
what no one even saw
often we don't consider what we can't see
but fine silk threads stretch north across the sky
for heavy wings to follow
and under sidewalks, city shoes,
a jungle dark as coal
lets down her hair

I love the panther, the great whooping crane
and what comes each morning
has come every morning
waking me
rumpling sheets
reaching for the day
the prayer, mantra,
in every shape, color
every glance or stride across the room
the breath
on every wing and paw.

## THE DRAGON

the dragon came
lay low down at the base of the mountains
hiding in the mist
hiding from us in the mist
that hung in our hills
motionless

 we gave up hunting for awhile
and merely listened
the sound of her breathing
we could hear it
in the small hour before the dawn
all was quiet for a time
our hearts grew still
as mountains

although it was but a brief moment
in the history of our people
we named it " breathing dragon....quiet hearts"
and when the mist would come
lie low down at the base of the mountains
the children played a game
of hearts and dragons
but the old ones would walk the streets
as if bitten by a dream
hungering for the dragon
breathing in the mist
that held them captive for a time

while their hearts
their hunting hearts
grew still
as mountains.

## FOR JESSIE

all afternoon it was about to storm
or it wasn't
all afternoon the wind blew
hard in from the West
or not at all
ravens and the others
made no plans
trees relied on memory
no one could be happy
I fell into a stupor on the couch
and almost didn't meet you
though I said I would

and when we met
you told the finest story I have ever heard
ever
with no lies at all

late afternoon the small storm broke
though there was hardly any rain
the air turned cool
and quiet
ease
came over us
it must have been your story
caused the storm to finally break
all those diamonds
slipping from your pocket as you spoke.

## GIVE UP DISBELIEVING

I am queen of a little known country
the pores of my body release perfume of a purple flower
also little known
in the afternoons I lie naked on my bed
allowing breezes from the valley below
to cool my skin
when I was king
I never did this

I came out from the clouds to join you
your seasons
your cities
to fall like mist on your soft cheeks
and with the wind
pull down your hair

go into your fields
bend down
kiss the earth
and in that quiet moment
give up disbelieving I am real.

PRAYER

Lord
I am 62 years old and not yet wise
or deep
or true
I am not kind
the way some folks wear kindness
as an ordinary fragrance
all day long
I am not bright
see the chickadees
bright as little stars
as they dance and flick
around the birdseed in the snow
tell me Lord
what more is there

so bring me to your table
sit me down
I will not rise until you bless me
touch me Lord
the way you must have touched this paperwhite
that just this morning
burst open
into small white flames
here at my kitchen table.

## THEY'RE COMING

they're coming
babies
children
pure as snowfall in the forest
they bring such quiet innocence into our lives
even the thought of it
will stop us in our tasks
we turn and look around the room at nothing
wondering
us old ones
who come out from rocks
and shadows in the trees
to step into a meadow of children
sunlight shining in the grass
fine as silky spider webs

we'll need another language to talk to them
new words
yellow words and pink
words that sound like laughing in the trees
and have a taste of honey

and when we take them in our arms
feel their breath across our cheeks
it seems to us
fragrant music has come into the room
lifts us lightly
in the air.

the air is cool this morning on the porch
flag grass, yucca, pinon, juniper,
and all the tiny bugs
who pirouette so perfectly in the air
even the sun
the great white sun
who claims dominion over everything
this side of the mountain
the world that seemed so constant and true
cast off the myth of constancy today
in favor of a wilder force
one that dropped the likes of you
exploding softly in my lap
with no respect for "constant"

I dreamed a moth of time stole you away
fed you slices of fine dynamite
the dim explosions coming from your heart
I know what they mean

the mullein sentry nodding by the porch
offers little comfort
but some advice
"let crack what will
explosions must occur
remember geodes from your youth
you found them in creek beds
by smashing open likely rocks
there they were
twinkling like the eyes of saints

tiny glowing crystals that
seemed to hold the world in place
allow the shattering
it is required
the little light
never did and never will
reveal herself
through any force
less terrible
and true."

## THE WONDER

can you see her
out there in the dark before the dawn
moving through the trees
one lone doe
legs like boney branches
her body hidden in the piney brush
her head, to me,
a queen or saint

can you see her there
outside the window
moving through the piñons
her steps deliberate and slow
as she walks off out into the forest
trailing mystery behind her

leaving us in this room of dawning light
with the mystery she brought
as though we ourselves
have stepped into the wonder forest
into an air ineffable and strange
yet wholly familiar
the deep unknown we know we come from
we recognize it as our own
our birthright
who we truly are

out there in the dark and trees
one lone doe
or saint

delivering us this morning
the wonder
the one true thing we live for

at times the only thing
to make us want to stay.

## FALL

in the heat of the day
when the air is sleepy
I walk my two dogs down to the corner tree
where horses in the shadows swish their tails
the small dark one looks up
as we pass by

but today the air is turning cool
leaves cadmium yellow
a faint scent of suffering
metallic
is in the air
it's Fall
Fall when sadness makes her home in me
for everything that's dying
leaves
grasses
my body
the warm air dies becoming cold
and every Fall
every single Fall
the migratory cells inside me wake up
"leave leave" they say
"time to go
dying is all around you
leave everything
this place
everyone you know
just go
O sister of sadness

sister of grief
walk into the mirror
go
make this sadness real"

## FOUR PALE COWS

*for Thomas and Colleen, their home in Texas*

four pale cows met me on the road
as I walked out this morning
as I walked out into the morning air
the live oak woods
four pale cows
we stopped
stared at each other
I wondered just how close
would they allow themselves to come
how close would I let them
and they were soft
cool and white as milk
but I was of a mind of love and heartache
having left behind the ones I love
to walk alone into the world
many days of heartache

so I turned walked up the road a little ways
and cut onto a narrow path
that led into the woods
seeking comfort from the trees
close comfort from the trees
pale winter grass
bright crackling leaves
distant ambiguities hidden in the branches
here I walked
but turning
there behind me on the path
four pale cows had followed me
it was their path
I knew it then
and stepped aside to let them pass

four pale bodies close together
moved as one along a path they knew
four moved as one along a path they knew
one hundred times they knew it
and left me standing
a stranger in the woods
alone

what makes a woman leave the ones she loves
leave all that's cherished daily
familiar
held very close to the bone
and walk away
walk off alone
it seems a drastic thing

yet here in this woods
this live oak woods
the shadows and the light
whistling birds and bellowing cows
the little wind that moves and lifts the winter grasses
here at last
in all that's still and moving
all that's still and moving
my heart reveals herself
shows her face in every leaf and twig
reveals how she alone is all the seeking
she all alone
the cure.

## SOFTER TIMES

I remember spanish moss hanging from the branches
in that fine old southern swamp
not far from Granny's house in Texas
and the road of sand we'd walk on down to get there
my feet have memories of that sand

I remember waking in the morning
to steady rain on the roof
quiet voices in the kitchen
and wondering what I'd do all day long inside the house
pecan leaves shining in the soft green rain outside the window
I want it back
the softness of that time
to feel the ease again.
It's gotten way too hard
too harsh
hard lines
hard moves
I want softness
inside me
all around me
a memory of rain
quiet voices in the kitchen
fine fine sand between my toes
my body round like a plum

white folks these days are sometimes frightened
by large bodies of softness
lets work on that
and when I die

don't burn me
lower my body down to my dark mother
that moist
black
softness
like chocolate cake
I never
ever
get enough.

## RETURNING TO THE LAND WHERE I WAS BORN
### —SOUTHEAST TEXAS

I looked and saw the land was flat
completely flat
there were woods, clearings, and
somewhere out there rivers
rolling down into the gulf
and all around the eye could see
the land completely flat

I rose
walked out the door
walked out onto the land
and stood there
I stood there on that land and I was whole
I stood there on that land where I was born
and I was whole
completely whole
wanting for nothing
nothing at all

I stood there on that land where I was born
and we were one
that land and I were one
as far around as the eye could see.

the Spaniards came to gather pine nuts
with their blankets, their babies
and camped beneath the piñon trees

Yolanda came
Yolanda of the night
offering me a cross and chain
silver in her almond hands
how could I refuse

the Mother led me to Yolanda
whose teenage son hitched a ride with me
right to her booth
silver and aquamarine
he and his father worked their mine outside of town
how could I refuse

I knew the day was meant for gifts
giving a full days wages for the chain
I knew the money was for her
the tiny shining cross for me

the Mother whispered it into being
the Mother whispered the exchange of silver
that day
in the market place.

## POEM FOR MY DAUGHTER

how often have I tried to write a poem for you
but words don't come
not ever

driving home today through the mountains
having spent three days with you
I watch the aspen leaves
tiny tambourines shaking in the wind
here and there
a blue spruce stands
primitive, alone in a clearing
precisely kind
I can say this
something of you moves in me
like water
like a river
and like all water
drives me down to the deepest place
where nothing moves
no sound
no word
is ever uttered
and holds me there
in the quiet of my heart
the way only a child
can hold a mother

I have no words for this
there are no words for water.

# LOVE POEM FOR MY THREE CHILDREN
## WRITTEN IN THE FALL

sometimes
watching you
chatting with a friend across the counter
or
watching you
loafing off down the alley
round the bend
or you
simply stooping down
to tie the red lace of your shoe
sometimes
a simple gesture
I look at you and know
you could disappear
vanish
suddenly
and not return
and grief
so merciless and fierce
a breath of it would fell a forest
could be breathing down on me
for none
of all that we hold close and dear and safe
are ever safe
in this fabric of a dream

the risk we take for love
for a hand we hold
and the bitter root
I take it for the three of you
and seize the chance to do so.

the moon hung in the peach tree leaves
a lemon slice in the sky
when the night was all about peaches
your birthday party on the porch
peaches on the grill
you
turning 30
how did that happen
you were my child
a little shooting star I could catch
and hold you in my arms
when you'd run into the room
these arms are empty now
limp with grief
a bitter moon wept with me for all my memories
I had little appetite for peaches

there must have been some force of grace
                              for mothers on the porch
for a moment I saw your boyhood face
I saw what I always see in your eyes
at 3, 4, or 30
you
regarding your world
a constant you among the people all around you
accountable
but only to the blazing elemental fire inside
claiming you entirely and exactly as you are
your only face
I saw it for a moment in the crowd

the sky is blue among the leaves this morning
birds attack the peaches still left on the tree
on a nearby roof pigeons land and settle
you'll wake
come join me on the porch
we'll talk about last night and smile
there will be peaches
singed a little in the fire
but this morning
aren't so hard to swallow.

coming home from town today we drove
into a snowstorm on the road
Max's teenage music blaring in the car
    " death...and rape...and I've got nothing more to say"
but coming from a voice so deeply soulful
I was surprised to hear the vocalist
was only 22

we drove out of the storm into a clearing
the road in front cut across the plains
the sky was low and white
all around prairie grasses and brush
were maize and mustard colored
giving off a golden light
the only light there was
as though a magic wand reached out
and touched the world
cast a golden spell on everything
this holy light felt different
than the pale blue light we're accustomed to

and it was everywhere
down the road
across the fields
shimmering in the air above the grass
it came into the car
on Max's arms at the wheel
his tee shirt
on his face
about to change forever

from a boy into a man
it made each thing about him
so distinct
yet soft
slightly golden
enchanted

we drove on through the afternoon
in this prayer of light
I could have driven on forever.

## ALONE IN THE DARK

alone in the dark I wait for you
your footsteps on the porch
the last of my three children still at home
memories of your childhood
tumble from my mind
like schoolchildren let out on the streets

but you're not coming home tonight
I know that now
no more late night vigils
are required of me
what will I do without you when you're gone
with all these memories
my body seems too big tonight
my tongue grown fat and hot
inside my mouth
no more vigils
and all these memories

O earth support me now
give me everything you give a tree
I am alone again
and feel a big one
coming on.

## SLEEP TALKING

sometime in the night I waken to his voice
coming through the dark
my son is talking in his sleep
to an invisible assembly gathered in his room
and I listen
an uninvited guest
not to the words
he speaks a language I never learned
but to the sound below the words
the sound his soul is making
effortlessly

so much rides in the voice
each time we speak we are constructed
and this night
this gentle bodied boy of 16
tells me
in gruff and tender speech
with no excuse or pretense
accountable
to no one
his soul is as accessible to him at night
as near
and recklessly companionable
as is the loose change
he carries in his pocket
by day

## ABUNDANCE OF EMERALDS.

*for my mother*

sunlight through the window
falls on orchid leaves
those floppy rabbit ears
each one with one hard line
that cuts clean up the middle
it turns each leaf a desperate green
desperate
that brilliant emerald light
just moved the mountain
that had settled on my heart last night
notice things as they are
they will give you
exactly what you need

the sunlight moves to cover me
wrapped in a blanket on the couch
my hands were resting in my lap
like winter cats
but now the left one gently strokes the right
silk and bones
I think it is my mothers' hand
come back to touch her child again
although how could it be
her left hand
always wore an emerald

again the sunlight moves
it leaves this room
progressing into a world of countless rooms

countless rooms
where mothers live and move
desperate lives will feel the light
for such a small amount of time
before it goes to light up
orchids
emeralds
light up all the emeralds of the world.

my father has grown more remote than ever
his mind turned wobbly like his legs
he can't remember what "before" means, or "next"
doesn't recognize me
he's like a tiny grain of sand on the beach
down where the waves come in
waiting for a big one
to take him out to sea

last night in my sleep I thought I heard him cry out
he's a thousand miles away
but I thought I saw him rise up in his bed
crying out

did a big one come
crashing down on him
force him to his knees
has my father been returned to simplicity
are his coat and shackles out there drifting on the water
and even as I write
is there a handful of gold medallions
sparkling in the sea light
settling now
settling to the bottom of the sea.

## FOR FELICIA   MY GRANDDAUGHTER
## 16 YEARS OLD, IN THE HOSPITAL

though you are beautiful it hurts to see you lying here
after the wicked surgery has made you empty
your hair limp weeds on the pillow
your arms, the swans,
tell a sad story of what I wasn't here to see
but can imagine

lacking strength now to conceal itself
your beauty lies on you
like a child lies on its mother
and like all innocents
unprotected
by anything but grace
rarely have I seen such grace

and all the while outside the door
down the hallway
drifting through this hospital of children
comes the Fan of Death
but
not to this room
not to this bed
for in your eyes
your eyes
as certain as the moment you were born
I see there still
in your eyes
your agreement to be here.

little prince
little cricket
dropped down to us from a distant star
down to earth
where we are heavy, dense, dull witted
even at our best
and slow to recognize a small bright thing
living here among us
how will you possibly adjust to us

and if we cleave to you
will you save us
from the daily torture of too much
and not enough of what is light
lightest
lacking gravity

little prince
tenderhearted
I see how you're moving through the world
your small body cleaving to an inner star
I would be like you
and
old though I am
old though I am
I will find a way.

## FOR MATEO   WHEN HE WAS A BABY

when I see your face
your smiling face
eyes of a thousand clowns light up in my mind
laughter floods my heart
you bring so easily the simple joy of life
which mostly we've forgotten

the look of you
love lights in your eyes
the shameless ecstasy of being
your gift to us
I take it home with me
a handsome prize
as I drive out tonight.

# JUSTICE

they're fighting in the house this morning
when I arrive
my son and his girlfriend
instead of eggs and toast
I get a bucket and mop
room full of wasps, broken hearts
and the terrible demand for justice

O my
the terrible demand
it wounds the heart a second time
rains down nails into the downy softness
ineffable sweetness
that gives itself to us from time to time
and in those moments
we are sure
that, after all
this is truly all there is

but the terrible demand for justice
cold black steels holds prisoners inside the house
and in the darkening room
morning plans do not include each other
the eye of love grows dim.

standing by the sink in my son's kitchen
the pots yell out to me
" wash me . . . wash me . . . we'll tell you about your son"
how he stands here moving pots from stove to sink
scrubbing out the bottoms
washing, rinsing, rinsing, dreaming
dreaming of the woman he has yet to meet
but always known
his body built for perfect union with his dream
the way our bodies dream at night
of rivers
valleys
hills
and slip into the landscape of their dreams

in his dreaming he drops a pot
lets out a little yell
outside the window on the street
a woman walking by
the woman he has yet to meet
but always known
hears the little yell
coming from the window
and dreams a momentary sidewalk dream
of two in love becoming one

so the clever pots achieve their dream
of the first meeting
here in this world
where so many share
a soft propensity to dream.

# A KING

*for Thomas, on hearing his dream*

he comes to us, this man
walking like a king
we see how he's become a king
moving through the crowd
like a star across the sky
aligned and undisturbed
we respond to his approach
by growing quiet

nothing more is happening here
no nothing more
the earth has made her choice
the earth has
entered him
stars called out his name
claim his flesh and blood
as their relation
no commentary necessary
no argument put forth
when the earth bestows
the man responds

there's a song that tells of an ancient covenant
between the earth and man and stars
a covenant to bind the three
the song begins to move now deep within the man
to rise, and swell, and take him like the sea
once more a king is born
to keep the covenant
once more a song
to keep a king.

# AN ARTIST

*for John who said he gave birth*
*to the guitar he made*

there was a guitar that made a man

a guitar so skilled
elegant
and quiet
it made a man to play on

and took him to the schoolyard
where he played among the children in the morning
took him to the town cafe at night
where he danced so hard on the wooden floor
blood poured through the soles of his shoes
tears streamed down his cheeks
violets bloomed in his teeth
and his heart pounded
like waves on the shore

so he took the man everywhere
played him for everyone
because he knew he made the right man
now he knew
he made the man
right.

## A MAN OF GOD

*for Patrick*

you left us
went out on the mountain
sat alone for more than 40 days and nights
though there was nothing we would do about it
we thought and thought of you
then you came back down
but changed
the you who left
did not return
we have a different you

what happened on that mountain
did something rise up in you
or fall away
did God take you away and
bring us back this different you
standing here in front of us
like nothing more than sunlight warming up the room
and moving through as lightly
as one moment moves into the next
and yet, in truth,
with you there's something more
abiding deep and quiet
as though you never left the mountain
you never left the mountain

we can't hold you anymore
you got too big

God
will hold you now.

transparent portrait of a queen
queen of orchids
elemental
proud
you there, not there
drapery in the chair
the history of moonlight on your forehead
tiara of the night sky round your head

from the outskirts of the heart we come
returning to our home in darkness
weeping for the deep remembrance
the final movement of the heart
the only movement left
while you
our highway into darkness
queen of all dark highways
all dark orchids
sit
there
not there
moonlight
in the chair.

# TRANSFORMATION

*for Brahmi*


a heap of jewels sparkling colors
dazzling in the desert sun
becomes too hot
bursts into flames
the flames are terrible and fierce
tongues of long forgotten angels
burn out all memory of what was there
a cry is heard in Heaven
and in the smoldering place
all that remains
a small white goblet
trembling on the ground

we're born we live we die
but when the fire walks through us
the dream that keeps us separate from the world
is burned away
and looking out
all we see is innocence
it is the cup from which we drink
drink deeply
of our own
sweet innocence.

## FOR COLLEEN

I live in the third world country of my body
my mind angry dictator
making war on me
I'm like a little rabbit
hiding deep inside the leaves
dreaming of the open fields
my poems are pebbles that mark a path
out of the brush

I sense
can almost feel out there
the millionaire sky
bending down to touch my fur
now quiet
victorious.

## EL PROFESOR

*for William*

who could have known
behind the mild, ministerial, and scholarly demeanor
of the professor
lives and breathes an actor
tonight *el rubio*
*el matador primo*
pacing, prancing across the stage
clicking his silver heels
magnetizing every coin of gold and silver in the room
every blushing rose and scrap of velvet
tossed up on the stage

who would have thought
behind the soft eyes
and liquid thoughts of the professor
lives and breathes an actor
tonight *el toro*
snorting, pawing the stage
commanding presence
commanding every heart to open
every eye to sigh
as we dared to watch
what no one dreamed would ever happen
*el profesor! el profesor!*
burning in an ancient fire
consumed by living flames
transformed into a diva
right before our eyes

no! professor no!
do not walk off the stage
retreating to your chambers
your books and thoughts
its way too late for that
you've gone too far

tonight you wrap us in your velvet cloak
reveal your secret flaming heart
and leave us
burning in your fire.

# BIRTHNIGHT

*for Shila*

he gave it to her
at her birthday dinner
a necklace
many small cut glass stones they were
pale green against her
soft pink skin

he gave it to her
a necklace
strands of milky green
hung around her throat
and shone
it lit her up
lit many fires inside her
burning to make her new
burning to make her all she was
it was her night her day her birth
and she was burning burning burning

he gave it to her
the necklace fell down from the ceiling
and hung around her throat
like a snake called forth from out the jungle
to wrap around this Finnish girl
who came to us from her land of ice and snow

and it was green, green, the mystery of green
green magic shone around her throat
and she was pink her eyes cornflower blue

and she was burning burning burning
to be all she was
burning to be new
it was her night her day
her birth
she was so pleased
she was so very pleased
she was so new
she shone.

her hair you'd notice first
it was bushy
long as a river
and full curls
she was tall and lean
and came to us from Kansas
was very colorful
and kept a steady beat of style

and she was bright
we all were bright
there at the table eating dinner
on into the night
so very bright
except for Nate
who sat there like a big white bear
big white stone
big white earthquake
big white moon
eating chocolate

she'd wanted some
searched cupboards, drawers,
it was gone
he ate it all
ate all the chocolate in the house

but I found chocolate in my heart that night
as I began to know to love
this tall lean curly girl
who came to us from Kansas
with hair
long as a river.

FOR CHEYENNE
LOCAL ACUPUNCTURE MASTER

should a raptor
all in white
fly in through your window
come to you on a beam of light
and ask you with her eyes
to let her peck you
pierce you with her beak
that you might feel
the little entries
thrusts into your body

would you let her
would you take a chance
that something wonderful
might happen.

## IRISH NORAH

Norah led me to the bottom of the house
a corner in the back
to a room more like a cave
where she goes to meditate and pray
hour upon hour in a chair made comfortable
with pillows and a heating pad
it sits before a wall she painted
dark emerald green
one silver cross hangs on the wall
it brought to mind the caves of distant hermits
she spoke about
their prayers, incantations
the lonely piping on the hills

something unexpected caught my eye
in the corner of the room
a presence nearly visible
suspended
it seemed to be there waiting
inviting Norah, beckoning her
to come beyond the walls
into the world within the world
perhaps she drew him to her from the wild
that very fine peculiar air

I stood there staring at the corner
reluctant to leave the lively presence
wondering does it ever happen
after hours and hours
Norah fastening in with prayer

or even after just a moment
a breath of unfamiliar air
do the doors of Norah's secret heart swing open
to the world within the world
to know all things through tenderness
to see how bright
to see not one
even one
ever stands alone
the very land of hearts' desire
does it happen in that room that cave
does he take her with him
in that fine
peculiar air.

SONGBIRD

*for Jillian*

I hear a bird singing in the morning
releasing every color hidden by the night
into the light of day
I hear it when you sing

I hear waves rush the shore
and the high cry of a hawk
I've heard what very well might be the sound a snail makes
moving in the secret dark
below the grass
and the silence that hangs in the air above the ground
where six feet under
bullets whips and lethal gas
disturb the roots of trees

I hear voices of people everywhere
just speaking with each other
love can be so simple
but most of all
coming from your throat
I hear a constant willingness to say it all
to say it true
bring us the sounds we yearn to hear
our sounds

I think the angels say
the human voice can become an instrument of God
you like a little bird just singing to the air
no longer ask permission.

# TRIBUTE TO THE PIANO PLAYER
### *for Annatta*

the woman with long arms
is playing her piano
from across the room
the piano her sweetheart her lover
we sit in chairs
hands resting in our laps
listening to the pounding
on the ivory and ebony

the woman with long arms
is playing her piano from behind the walls
the piano her lover her soul mate
saying
tell them please exactly
what they are

they are the rivers and river rocks
lying in the moonlight on the shore
they are the baby leaves of trees
opening in their mothers' arms
they are the ache and howling cry
the earth rocking in the night
they are the little mirrors of themselves
they always knew they were
they are the moment of breaking open
to the one ecstatic violin
playing in their hearts

the woman with long arms playing her beloved
is awakening in them the memory of
exactly what they are.

he walked across the dining room
stood beside our table
across from us
across from me
I think he knew that I was watching
saw what I was seeing
felt how I was feeling
and so he took a chance
caught the wave
and danced into a momentary field of love

the air grew bright
his hips turned left turned right
his arms withdrew
head came through
wrists a twist
his eyes
blue eyes
were little cups of love

so we watched
we watched him take a chance
catch the wave
and dance us all
into a momentary field of love
there beside the table
in that
dining room of life.

it came to me one night
it was the way
she said her name
as though she were a stranger to herself
and full of possibilities
any one of which might open
right in front of her
as she walked around a corner
or stop her for a moment
like a dream
suddenly remembered in the middle of the day

I like it like this
moving the day like a river
like a sweet song

and all that really matters
is happening.

## LOVE POEM

I have an odd
an intimate request
send me one of your old shirts
well worn
whose cloth by now will contain
the countless little sighs your body has been making
year after year
when I'm brave enough
I'll put it on

because I know that when I do
your arms
fingers
chest
the brute and tender force of you
captive in that shirt
will all at once
recognize and want to touch
my naked
breathless
skin.

## REFUSAL

today since you
the one I love the most
refuse to speak to me
none
of this world's beauty
will I accept
but the lonesome calling of the morning dove
from her small hollow throat

I hear it now dropping through the leaves.

# MORNING WALK ENCHANTMENT
## ANNE SILVER'S WOODS

who went walking
who went walking with them
into the morning light
the forest air
down to the Cedars
and stood in the thoughts of aging branches
and knew the world through kinship with a tree

who went walking
who went walking with them
down to the cunning creek
sat and stared into the water
beguiled to surrender
to join the glassy realms
and give all the rest away

who was green and who turned golden
under the arcing sky
stood in the grass the light and shadows
the warm medallions of the sun
heard the birds and saw the branches
rising up from trees
who make us more than we are
stepped on stones that never move
and walked into a careful closet of small trees
where neck bones of an elk
lay on the ground
in a graceful arc
white like stars laid out across the heavens

who went walking in the morning meadow light
yet stopped, turned, walked away
to live enclosed, shut off in houses
blinded by walls that give back
none of all they hide away
who turned away from the hearts of birds
the ancestral cloak of trees
away from the diamond life

and who remained behind
with footprints in the grasses
and with eyes.

## THE GIFT

my neighbor left her Christmas porch lights on tonight
no shining star of Bethlehem blazing in the sky
but rows of tiny fireflies strung together
lighting up the cold night air
the light comes through the window upstairs
where I'm lying in the dark
it mingles with the black
some things are shown
others, still fallen back in darkness

eventually we all come to the same conclusion
this   THIS  is all there is
holy moment
pause
rolling in from eternity
on out into the night

the way that children come to us
lean into us for love
we turn and lean into the soft night air
the promise
and without quarrel give the little we have left
to find that
what remains
is all we ever wanted.

we are wolves of the forest
we are birds of the morning air
we are wind in the grass
and dark river water
we are flowers that close their petals
in the soft green evening light

we are storms out at sea
and fire in the canyon
we are stars that sing in the rivers of night
we are birds of the morning air

from all around and deep within
from every stone, petal, leaf and wing
a voice is calling calling us
wooing wooing us
opening a door
for some sweet moment
when without memory or thought
stepping through
we know that we are here
and know how we are here
to love this world
to love this
daring life.

what used to be my heart is now a meadow
wide open to receive the world
every tree, bush, stone,
each little breeze and every star
is reaching out to me
offering itself
inviting me to know we are the same
same substance
different form
and we belong
we belong together
we are held in an embrace of love
so utterly without reserve
the like of which I've never known
and never knew I could

the skin of God is on my eyes
and like a woman on her deathbed
or a child
I see the world just as it is
as it has always been
offering itself
a field
an open meadow
where everyone is welcome
no one is excluded
and no one
no one ever
in this world
is forgotten.

## I SUBMIT

I submit to sunlight coming in the room
through thin yellow curtains
each leaf of every plant
is greener than it was
I submit to final moments in the dim light
as secrets of the room
rush to disappear

and now I know
tea cup in my hand
sweetness in my mouth
thighs heavy on the couch
warm against the little dog
resting next to me
now I know
this is how it's going to be
always how it's going to be
particulars will change
room to room
life to life
but nothing else will
no
nothing ever will.

this morning as the sun rises behind the mountain
I watch the light on the top peaks
begin to roll down ridges
and for a moment
something
in me
rises up to meet the light
as though I am the mountain
I am the mountain for a moment
and that's enough
there it is
the world that seemed so fragmented
reveals itself as whole
nothing more is needed
love is everywhere
in everything
beneficent
I am home

how often in an ordinary quiet moment
the magnificence will reveal itself
and almost always
through the smallest movement possible.

## SEEING YOU

*for Mark*

I hope one day to see you
standing here in front of me
wide open
like a morning on a highway
that brought you here
perhaps you will have made
difficult, slender movements in your mind
to make it possible for you to come

and as a miner stepping out to work one day
who finds the entrance to the mine has been shut down
will drop his tools
and with them
all he ever held
perhaps when you see me
we both will feel the history we carry
the sudden weight of all our histories
drop from us to the ground
like massive shelves of arctic ice
I once saw in a film
break from the mainland
and slip thundering
slo-mo
into the sea.

## MICKEY PARADISE

Mickey Paradise crossed the river
didn't look back
not even once
all the cells of my body
cried out to go with him
but I didn't move
something strong
stronger than the river
held me back
though my heart froze like a bird in the snow

Mickey P crossed the river
my heart froze
something strong I don't know what but it took hold of me
and holds me still

a person can look in a thousand directions
and see only one thing.

sunlight through the lilac leaves
dapples the side of my neighbors' barn
and the air is cool this morning
as the magpie journeys through

don't you wish you could be the sunlight
dappling the barn
don't you wish you could be the air
caught in the wings of the sudden bird

be still
listen
something will tell you
something inside already knows
the sunlit faces of all your cells
are
dappling the barn
the rhythmic beating inside your breast
is
the windy wings of the blackbird

you can live this way
in fact you were born to
release your fears from their little cages
the time has come
to receive the ghost.

FOR AARON ABEYTA AND HIS NOVEL
                    —RISE, DO NOT BE AFRAID

did
one day
perhaps when you were young
the earth knock at your door
say
"come, I have chosen
you will be my instrument, my horn
I will play and you will make the notes
the golden tones
that cause them to remember all they love
but have forgotten that they love

the wind blowing round the corners of the house
and out there causing dust storms in the field
the earth below their feet
warm from having baked
all day long in the oven of the sun
little stones beside the road
quietly recording their lives
ravens black cries high up in the trees
and cottonwoods
groves of priestly elders
where anyone can go for comfort
anyone who may have
taken things too far
and water
always water
telling tales boiling in their pots
pelting down on them like silver nickles from the sky

as they dash inside the house
always the little melodies water makes
that seep into their skin
find where they are hiding
and change their minds

and you my horn
when you sleep at night
trees outside your window
will move in close
and come into your dreams
at dawn the chattering of small birds falls from your lips
some sounds will come so easily you forget that you are real
other sounds will make it
hard to breathe

but you will make the symphony they hear
and cause them to remember all they love
from the morning sun
warming them in every room
to the moonlight
soft across their sheets at night

hearing they remember
in that moment of remembering
who knows
you may see them rise."

## EASE

this morning I waken to an ease a sweetness
that wasn't here the night before
when the management of life
felt burdensome, comfortless

the air now soft and sweet
as though spring crocuses were hiding somewhere
blooming in my room
and little elves had entered in the night
and cleaned for me

such unexpected ease
no rush to get things done
no push
or shove
no cause to take
or demand that anything be different than it is
just ease

I wish I felt this all the time
comfort without cause
like a fragrance in the air
rising from the earth
warm and generous
entering through every pore

as though I'm standing in a little boat
on a river
catch the water's current
feel the swell around the boat

rise up through my legs into my arms
I stand here gently gliding through the water
watching down the river for what may come
a little breeze across my cheek
just enough
to tell me where I am.

# I FORFEIT ALL I THOUGHT I KNEW

when a yearning rose up in me
to be among the faerie folk
and the ancient ones moving dimly in the mist
I came here to this hill
gathered up the emerald air around me
and slipped myself into the mist

and the old ones came
rushing up to me
dark hands petting stroking me
eagerly reclaiming one returned to them
they offered me a large white chair
and went about their ways

the world beneath the world
land of a hidden sun
entered me on this dry hill
I forfeit all I thought I knew
above
below
two worlds have come together
to make a whole
a seamless world
at last the hand fits in the glove

I never felt like this before

the wind moves in the cedar boughs
and all is forfeit
what I thought I knew.

# THE BELOVED

at the center the core of my being
a great bird is winging its way into the sky
one eye trained on the moon
for a compass
round the throat of the bird on a golden chain
my heart hangs like a locket
endlessly stroking the sky
these two traveling companions press on
one eye on the sun for forgiveness

this is no koan
no koan
this is my heart and its beloved
whose love for each other
has created the sky
this journey on wings
these simple traveling instructions:
for love of the infinite in all things
make room
keep one eye in the light of the sun
give the other one to the moon
and never
forsake the beloved.

so
at last
I meet myself
know now what I am
ask no one for advice

because
last night
I went a little mad
drank from a crazy bowl
rules, definitions
tumbled from my mind like dice
till no thought held significance
no compass pointed north
fear came with boney fingers tapping at my ear
whispering this time I'd gone too far
no touch would bring me back
but out there on that spinning coin
without introduction
rose up in me the one thing
I could never lose
impossible impossible to lose
myself
I met myself

I am seer poetess
one of the old ones
the shy dark ones who dream the earth
I live in trees
cut the cord

water is my nature
rippling lakes
the creeks
and I have owls for eyes
if you dare ask
I'll dance for you
and you will know your fate
I am seer poetess
I whirl alone
perhaps I'll chose to grow my hair
long as the wind
who swells and reaches out in darkness for the stars

last night I went a little mad and met myself
I'm  pleased to say I dwell within
and never can be lost
never can be lost.

## THE WUNDERLING

*to accompany John Reeves sculpture*

mine is the face of a wunderling
people look at me and smile
like
something wonderful is happening
clouds lifting from their hearts

they walk down the street
in their coats and hats
and look into each other's eyes as they pass by
smiles coming to their lips
a thing so dear
so wonderful is happening
could never be forgotten

mine is the face that tells them so
people look at me and smile.

## OUT FROM THE MOON

*to accompany John Reeves' video of his sculptures*

out from the moon
from the center of the moon
from the calendar of stars in your eyes
the footprints of time
comes the sound the voice
of the One

as dark turns to light
you stand on the earth
you stand in your circle of ground
in the ground
in the grass
all the patterns of earth
your companions for life
and as light turns to dark
from center to rim
you stand on the earth
while your soul is caressed by the creature of time
as the creature of time
is caressing  your soul
feel the breath
of the One
in your face.

## CHERRY BLOSSOMS

cherry blossoms on the road
cherry blossoms
wind
blew them in my face
and I had thoughts
dreams
of you
in that pink dress
that little
dress
of yours

O sweet sister
take me in
I'm too long out here
dreaming in the wind.

hold me
hold me
hold me now
soft morning air
as I'm waking in this room
this bed
this morning light
hold me
hold me
hold me here soft air
the way sky holds clouds
rivers hold their banks
birds' cry holds the tops of trees

hold me
hold me
hold me now
soft  air
soft morning air
as I'm falling from the rivers of the night
into this room
this bed
this waking life
keep me
keep me
keep me here
soft air
hold me to this place.

pine trees
ravens
bugs in the dirt
birds calling across the mountains, the meadow, the sky
Rinpoche came to America
with his baggage of Dharma
and out of the bag stepped
imperial
queenly
jewel of nakedness
Dharma
on the spot we were given permission to be ourselves
on the spot we were given permission to be nothing
now we are free to use our eyes
our eyes are now free to use themselves
and so I have seen you
beautiful bird
plumed with the wildest colors
you strut you peek you perch you peck
you imagine yourself surrounded by things
but I am a mirror for your magnificent self
I love you
I long for you
shy and embarrassed I hide from you
but we are both mirrors
loving and longing
is emptiness and compassion
it's the sound of the conch blown across the meadow
as Rinpoche slips into the clouds
leaving this place forever

no more will we see his shining face

hearts turn to stone now
stones that can weep
stones that have wings
stones with bright arrows
stones with protection cords
stones that aren't stones
we are jewels of nakedness
slipping in
to the bag
of the
Dharma.

## TRAVELLING ALONE IN WINTER

travelling alone in winter
on a road through fields of frozen leaves, frozen grass
waking to deeper Mondays
on a road borne on and on into the mist
like a song that never ends

driving in the cold
days and days
the promises of Tuesdays never come
dreams desires pass by
like road signs into nowhere

but one who goes alone on roads may meet
a mysterious and beautiful companion
of travelers on the road
an angel
an angel of all alone
all alone and golden
riding there beside you
suddenly you know, you feel
how truly, deeply, nakedly
alone you are
and all the world
the wide wide world
moves in close
and intimate
trees, brush, fields along the road
lose their distant look
the heart beating in your breast
drops down to find its deeper home

and you remember what you may have forgotten:
you are familiar with the Infinite

it is holding, holding you
the way a mother holds her child
speaking to you, murmuring, breathing
breathing you
the way a mother breathes the child she holds

on roads these deeper roads that lead nowhere
where dreams, desires won't be met
the all alone
the Infinite
and oh so intimate
may come  for you

when nothing else will.

the ponies on the top of the hill
live in the wind
and are silhouetted by the mountains
spotted and black in the snow
they move about
with nothing but the sky
on their shoulders
frosty breath
dust
yucca
fur
things on the top of the world
are dry and singular
so intimate
and vast

I meant to tell you that I love you
that I'm leaving
but the words were too big
or too small
laid out across my life

now all we have are words
they come like
snow falling
in the mountains.

www.ingramcontent.com/pod-product-compliance
Lightning Source LLC
Chambersburg PA
CBHW071641050426
42443CB00026B/798